Taking Steps in Loss and Life

Guided Reflections Journal

By Barbette Shepherd
Coauthored by Randy Shepherd

Copyright ©2013 by Barbette and Randy Shepherd

All rights reserved. No part of this publication may be reproduced in any form without written permission from Barbette or Randy Shepherd.

ISBN-13:
978-1494308018

ISBN-10:
1494308010

This journal is an excellent aid in accomplishing grief work. It is not intended to take the place of the services of a licensed, competent professional. The foundational approach is based on the findings of experts and research regarding all content herein. All efforts have been expended to cite acknowledgments of influential works.

Other books by the authors include *Taking Steps in Loss and Life: A Grief Support Group Manual* and *The Parable of the Gardener: For Those Who Grieve*. Visit their website to learn about on-ground and tele-opportunities offered through LifeSteps: Shepherds' Integrative Services at www.lifesteps.us / Lifesteps@outlook.com.

Dedication

This is for all human beings who experience the sorrowful afflictions of grief; past, present, and future.

Taking Steps in Loss and Life: Guided Reflections Journal

CONTENTS

Introduction 1
    A New Understanding of Grief 1
    The Work of Renewal 2
    The Energy of Pain and Anger 2
    Conversations with Self 2
    The Benefits of Guided Reflecting 2
    Processing Emotions 3
    A Holistic Approach 3
    Verbal Guided Reflections 4
    You Are Unique 4

Reflection Sets 5
    Emotion Drawings 5
    Processing Feelings 7
    Looking Closely at Your Loss 11
    Remembering 13
    Write a Poem or Letter Addressed to Death 15
    Contemplating Meaning 17
    Recalling Personal Strengths 19
    Danglers: Unfinished Business 23
    Making Decisions 25
    Write a Letter of Sympathy to Self – Write a Truce with Self 29
    Adjusting to Newness in You; in Your World, and in Relationships 31
    Moving Ahead 33

Reflections Revisited 37

Emotion Drawing Section 55

Appendices 65
    A) The Grief Realm 66
    B) Comforting Scriptures 67
    C) Be Quiet Death! 68

About the Authors 69

References 71

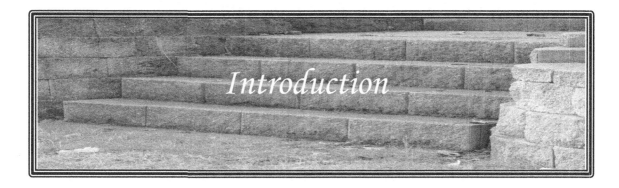

Introduction

Congratulations on taking a step toward renewal in the face of loss. A great deal of care for you, the griever, has gone into composing this reflection guide. Think of it as having been written for you personally. In acquiring a copy of this book, you've gained a personal guide to assist you in processing your grief. This book was designed either to be used unaccompanied or with a *Taking Steps in Loss and Life: Grief Support Group*. Should you feel the desire to unite with others in the grief journey, we invite you to visit the LifeSteps Coaching website at www.lifesteps.us for information concerning our teleconference support groups.

A New Understanding of Grief

Reassuring comfort is found in knowing the reflection question sets provided throughout this book are not just arbitrary. Instead, they have been designed to advance healing as they guide you through the designated tasks of grieving (Worden, 2009). Through research, experts have discovered there is much more to processing grief than older models have depicted. Grief stages of denial, anger, bargaining, depression, and acceptance (as first acclaimed by Elizabeth Kubler-Ross, 1969) are but small parts of the process a griever will undergo! Contemporary principles convey grief can be best managed by working through tasks involving regular self-care and attention. Upon looking inward, you may discover yourself dealing with any number of these undertakings at a time. You also may find you need to go back and revisit some of the tasks as you come into new self-discoveries through your reflection work. The questions presented in each reflection set stir awareness of what may need a closer look and where you may need to apply efforts toward healing. As you work though the journal, you'll begin to work through the five primary tasks of grief as they are described in *The Work of Renewal*.

The Work of Renewal

1. Examine and treat the grief wound holistically; process the pain.
2. Allow the actuality and certainty of the death.
3. Reshape and nurture your bond with the loved one in your heart and memories.
4. Make effort to find or create meaning in the death.
5. Permit the death to re-define you in newness and growth, both inside and out.

(Hoy, 2007; Wolfelt, 2003; Worden, 2009)

Let the journal be your private outlet and your handbook to stay on track as you become enlightened about navigating *The Grief Realm (see Appendix A)*. Each question is a stepping stone in the path progressively guiding your journey toward renewal.

The Energy of Pain and Anger

Through personal experience, you've come to understand that emotional energy produced by pain or anger can be a powerful agent in disrupting wellness in life. This type of emotional energy can stay with a person for a lifetime if it's not processed appropriately in a productive way. The processing of pain and anger can occur through a variety of avenues. Simply put, we need to transfer what's on the inside to the outside in order to lessen or break the hold of emotional energy (Hoy, 2005). Words provide a passageway for this transference to occur. "Words are to the spirit as medicine is to the body" (Shepherd, 2013). You are about to embark on a pathway paved with words that can lead you toward an exit gate in *The Grief Realm*.

Conversations with Self

Typically, people express feelings and thoughts through conversations with others in order to gain understanding. Taking time to funnel thoughts inward and engage in self-conversation is also a powerful mode for uprooting and managing emotions. Self-conversation can lead to new realizations. Tackling grief thought by thought, in set increments helps break down an overwhelming, oppressive force into smaller manageable parts (Wolfelt, 2003; Worden, 2009). Hurtful encounters with grief can sensitively be given care eventually producing healing and new growth. New buds appear in the way of personal insights that sculpt self-understanding. Self-understanding gives a griever permission to be patient with themselves while grief wounds knit together. Patience and understanding are your protective coverings.

The Benefits of Guided Reflecting

While impromptu journal writing brings about some benefits, research shows *guided* journal writing brings about much greater restorative rewards (Neimeyer, 2012). The benefits of reflecting are enhanced when it's performed within a framework of thought-provoking information and questions. After all, it stands to reason if you know what to look for; you are more likely to find it. If you can get clear sight of the path to renewal, you can recognize when you're on it and when you're not. When you've finished the journal, it's hoped you'll be enriched with a greater awareness of all that's occurring to you in *The Grief Realm*.

Every reader will finish in a different place on their healing journey, and it's not expected you'll finish in a completely healed state. Grief wounds never leave us entirely; instead, they transform into life scars (Wolfelt, 2003; Worden, 2009.) The wish is for you to become strengthened and better able to manage the intensity of grief. It's hoped that new understanding will carry you through future grief surges that may still arise. Experts share three prominent markers of healing: The pain of grief will be felt minimally (Worden, 2009), you'll be able to re-invest into living in the moment, and you'll develop the capability to devote emotional energy into your new life and into new relationships (Grant, 1995).

Processing Emotions

What happens when emotions are processed? When something is being deliberately processed, it's being moved toward a goal through a series of actions or activities. Each action along the way alters the original form to some degree. The end form becomes different from the initial form. The same definition applies to emotions and grief. Processing emotions involves deliberate actions that produce renewed outcomes. Think of a diamond in its original rough form and picture what it looks like after it's processed! This is a great visual to keep handy. With work, your spirit can become solid, bright, and clear reflecting the life that surrounds you.

A well-known adage tells us *time heals all wounds.* This may hold some truth, but is it best to use time alone to heal a wound when there are so many helpful remedies available? Time alone doesn't prevent a wound from festering or worsening while waiting for healing to take place. A grief wound responds to emotional treatment and balms when given regular attention just as a physical wound responds to medicine and daily care. Guided reflecting is a form of caring for your wounded self. Think of processing grief as being similar to treating a wound. It is cleansed, nursed, and bandaged. Bandages are removed; the wound is examined, and the process is repeated. The hope is for the wound to continue to heal steadily without complication.

Processing emotional life wounds occurs in re-defining and refining thoughts and feelings to become more palatable. The results of this process include heightened awareness, self-understanding, and acceptance. One desired outcome of processing grief emotions is for you to experience a transformation from pain to a newly characterized emotional energy; an energy that can be re-invested into newness in life. A recommended short read for a beautiful imagery of this process can be found in the book *The Parable of the Gardener: For Those Who Grieve.*

A Holistic Approach

The first task listed in *The Work of Renewal* is, "*Examine and treat the grief wound holistically; process the pain.*" This step is intentionally listed first with the primary aim that you can begin to strengthen your ability to care for all aspects of yourself effectively as you move through *The Grief Realm.* The human essence is enveloped in five domains:

Spiritual, Physical, Emotional, Behavioral (Relational), and Mental (Thinking)

Grief impacts you in all areas of humanness, and all areas need care while you invest in healing. Holistic self-care needs to continue while you're in the vulnerable, stressful state of grieving. Guided reflecting helps you tend to grief's impact in all of these domains as you give deliberate focus to each one in answering the questions. A few reminders have been interspersed to prompt stretching in your reflections. In addition, research reveals the intensity of strength in a person's faith is linked to their resilience in life's challenges particularly in the shattering that strikes with grief. A list of popular scripture references has been provided in the Appendices in hopes they will fortify your spiritual domain.

Verbal Guided Reflecting

You may be among the customary group of people who don't enjoy writing in a journal. If you're able to keep your focus on the healing agents found in writing, it may become worthwhile to you. Even minimal writing has its rewards. However, if writing is out of the question for you personally, *verbal* guided reflecting can be an alternate outlet for you. Responses to the reflection questions can be recorded and kept in a private file on your computer or on a flash drive. Working through the question sets verbally, while reflecting internally, can be fruitful in healing. The key is to reflect deeply and privately, with an intentional focus. In both forms of reflecting, written or verbal, words are still being used for conversations with self to foster understanding and new perspectives. If you're participating in a *Taking Steps in Loss and Life Grief Support Group*, verbal reflecting will also prepare you adequately for the weekly sharing time. It might be beneficial to jot down just a few of your key insights as they surface.

You Are Unique

Finally, keep the comforting thought close by that your experience through grief is individually unique to you. There is no one right way to grieve, and there is no fixed amount of time that's acceptable (Wolfelt, 2003; Worden, 2009). It is known grief episodes can be peppered with periods of numbness and confusion wherein reason fades to the background. Emotional sneaker waves can overtake grievers out of the blue, catching them unaware. Be assured it's possible to move through this time of devastation successfully. Sometimes, grievers need a little help in finding their way. If your grief case is complicated, prolonged, or severe, it's always best to check with a competent, licensed professional to see if additional help is needed. Always be certain to participate only on a level that you feel comfortable when answering the questions and performing the activities in this journal.

Reflection Sets

Emotion Drawings

*I*t's advantageous to introduce you to *Emotion Drawings* here at the beginning of your guided reflection sets so you're prepared to use these right away. Emotion Drawings are a wonderful outlet for when words are hard to find. There are a few pages in the back of this journal designated for your drawings. You'll need some crayons or colored pencils. Your drawings might include shapes, scribbles, words, or expressive colors selected to represent best your feelings at the time of expression.

The drawings are most effective if you take a few moments to center yourself before beginning. Close your eyes, and focus inside of your heart and your mind. Give yourself permission to feel and to go into any pain that is present. Explore what you're feeling as your thoughts drift. Which thoughts connect to which feelings? Try to match your colors and crayon/pencil pressure to your emotions. Give close attention to emotions that are intense. Write a few words on each drawing if you desire. The words don't have to be in sentence form. Use this expressive exercise to close out any particularly sensitive or intense reflecting experience you encounter. Use the page that follows for your first drawing.

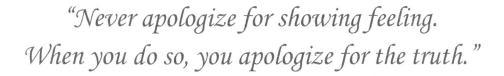

"Never apologize for showing feeling.
When you do so, you apologize for the truth."

(Benjamin Disraeli as quoted by Genn, 2013)

Emotion Drawing

Taking Steps in Loss and Life: Guided Reflections Journal

Processing Feelings

The first task in *The Work of Renewal* is, *"Examine and treat the grief wound holistically; process the pain."* This question set centers on the feelings at the hub of your wholeness. As you develop self-care strategies for tending to your emotional state, you'll be strengthened to perform the remaining tasks in your grief journey. It's a natural human instinct to try to avoid pain, yet in accomplishing grief work, you need to spend time visiting with your pain in order to work through it. Use the following questions to guide you as you begin thinking about your feelings, and processing them.

It takes courage to deal with the energy that builds up from intense emotions. Try to identify linking triggers or surroundings that evoke stronger emotions. If you can identify triggers, you'll facilitate a deeper awareness and understanding of your emotional state and begin to recognize the conditions that increase intensity. Regular exercise obtained in transferring inner to outer builds your emotional muscles. If it's revealed, it can be relieved; if it surfaces, it can be soothed. Revisit this reflection set regularly throughout the entire process of navigating *The Grief Realm*.

■ Right now, take a look inside, and try to identify your feelings. What are they?

_____
_____
_____
_____
_____
_____

■ Identify the feeling that tends to emerge the most often.

_____
_____
_____
_____

- Identify the feeling that tends to emerge the most intensely.

- Identify your surroundings when the feelings emerge.

- Identify the circumstances (triggers) when your feelings emerge.

- Identify the thoughts you are having when the feelings emerge.

- Identify what soothes your feelings and think of what may help you physically. Start implementing these actions into your daily and weekly routines if you haven't done so already. Suggestions may include long walks, hot baths, plenty of rest, aromatherapy, calming tea, and more. Make time for de-stressing activities and pay close attention to your physical care during this difficult time.

___

- Identify what can help you express your feelings. Be creative and think about a variety of avenues of expression that would really work for you.

___

- Let yourself think about how you would like to feel. Write down all the words that come to mind, even if they seem like a distant goal.

___

- Do you believe it's possible to feel this way again? Set your sights on these words, and let them be a beacon for you. Graciously offer kindness and acceptance to yourself as you perform the work of grief and push forward in finding your way.

Cathartic Clapping
(adapted from Neimeyer, 2012)

This is an exercise you can perform regularly as you continue to move your thoughts and feelings from the inside to the outside. Follow the instructions below, and journal your experience when you have finished with the exercise.

Instructions

Find a private setting, and get seated.
Center your focus on your pain, frustrations, stress, whatever is bubbling inside of you.
As you focus your thoughts, begin rhythmic clapping in a manner that
feels comfortable to your arms.
Try to extend your hands at least two feet apart between claps.
Let yourself feel the sensation that builds in your palms and fingers,
and connect these sensations to your thoughts.
Continue clapping for several minutes while maintaining your focus.
When you stop, sit quietly for a moment resting your hands in your lap.
Take notice of your renewed state of mind and of how the clapping may have
helped you process.

Looking Closely at Your Loss

*T*he second task listed in *The Work of Renewal* is, "Allow the actuality and certainty of the death." Taking time to look intentionally at your loss, increases understanding of how it's currently impacting you (Rich, 2001). As is sometimes the case, there may one or two areas in your grief that will protest repeatedly as you attempt to let go and close them. As you look inward, focus on areas that still feel unresolved. Is there anything particularly tough or complicated? If so, focus on the support available to you and give direct attention to how you might work through these barriers. With new discoveries attained from reflecting, clouding and uncertainty lessen their holds making way for new information and perspectives. With healing, comes clarity and strength for moving forward.

■ Write a few words expressing thoughts and feelings that apply to unresolved aspects you've come across in your grief journey.

_____
_____
_____
_____
_____
_____

■ Write about the specific details that tie into this unsettled area of grief.

_____
_____
_____
_____
_____
_____

■ Reflect on past losses in your life. What steps did you take to resolve these and to process your grief? How did you come through them? In what ways might these losses be complicating your current grieving process?

_____
_____
_____
_____
_____
_____
_____
_____

■ What are some helps available to you for sorting through any barriers to healing?

_____
_____
_____
_____
_____
_____

■ What are some steps you can take to cultivate adjustment or acceptance for these aspects of your loss?

_____
_____
_____

■ Direct your words to your loved one, and tell them of your struggles. If appropriate, comment on what you think they would want for you now.

_____
_____
_____
_____

Remembering

The third task listed in *The Work of Renewal* is, "*Reshape and nurture your bond with the loved one in your heart and memories.*" Writing is a fantastic way to capture history and shared life. Putting energy into memories helps to reshape the relationship bond that will forever remain. Use the following question set to journal this week and continue to revisit this section as other memories arise. Practice keeping a balanced view of your beloved. Reflections on memories can and should include some negative features right along with the positive. Know you have permission as a human being to possess both tender and thorny memories of one person, and that both can co-exist within the sphere of love. Indeed, love is even more evident when it persists in spite of challenges. Put some of your memories on paper so you can tuck them away in a safe place with the reassurance of never forgetting. This reassurance allows you to move forward knowing you will continue to honor the life that was lived.

■ What are some of the more fond, significant, or powerful memories you have involving your lost one? These may have occurred in the intimacy of a shared conversation, in a special celebration, or even in everyday life.

_____
_____
_____
_____
_____
_____
_____
_____
_____
_____

■ What were you feeling in each of these occasions?

_____
_____
_____
_____
_____

■ What, in each of these memories, characterizes your relationship with the one you lost? Give an answer for every memory you recalled. Your relationship with your beloved has many facets. Try to answer with a well-rounded, all-embracing thinking.

_____
_____
_____
_____
_____
_____
_____

■ Write a sentence or two to your loved one about each memory.

_____
_____
_____
_____
_____
_____
_____
_____
_____
_____
_____
_____

Write a Poem or a Letter Addressed to Death

This reflection exercise is designed to help you re-gain a sense of control over a formidable force in life. Write a poem or a letter addressed to *Death*. Review the poem *Be Quiet Death* (see Appendix B; Shepherd, 2013) as an example of what can be written. Spend some time in reflection, and identify what *Death* has taken from you and what death will not take from you. Tell *Death* what you think of it. As you work, notice if you are able to reshape your focus toward what remains rather than toward what was lost. Follow up your writing with an *Emotion Drawing*. Apply colors and shapes to your paper as extensions of your feeling palette. When you are finished, label the drawing, *A Letter to Death*.

_____
_____
_____
_____
_____
_____
_____
_____
_____
_____
_____
_____
_____
_____
_____
_____
_____

Contemplating Meaning

The fourth task listed in *The Work of Renewal* is, *"Make an effort to find or create meaning in the death."* Creating meaning from randomness or chaos is a basic human need, and human beings possess an incredible ability to do just that. From tragedy, people are able to bring about meaningful elements, which ultimately benefit themselves and others (Grant, 1995). In accomplishing this task, the memory of the death is linked strongly to a component of significance; one is not thought of without the other. Working through this step, you can bring understanding and peace within reach. Spend time pondering the questions below. See if you are able to begin to reframe the loss in a new way. Note ideas when they come to mind as making meaning may need to transpire over a period of time. Keep patience close by and take the time you need. Remain open to impressions and inspiration for accomplishing this step.

■ What do you value in life? Prioritize your list by importance.

_____
_____
_____
_____
_____
_____

■ What beliefs, convictions, principles guide you through each day?

_____
_____
_____
_____
_____
_____

■ What actions do you perform each day that hold meaning for you? What else continues to provide meaning for you?

_____
_____
_____
_____
_____
_____
_____

■ In what ways do memories of your loved one provide meaning in your life?

_____
_____
_____
_____
_____
_____
_____

■ How have your views of meaningfulness in life changed with this experience of death?

_____
_____
_____
_____
_____
_____

■ Direct your writing to your loved one. Write about the meaningfulness you've shared and how you might find meaning in your life now.

_____
_____
_____
_____
_____
_____
_____

Taking Steps in Loss and Life: Guided Reflections Journal

Recalling Personal Strengths

𝒰se this special reflection set for self-care in the midst of your grief work and for nurturing confidence as you push ahead navigating *The Grief Realm*. To begin your reflecting, take a moment to look at the map provided in the appendices. Try to determine where you are in your journey, and pay particular attention to how far you've come. Congratulate yourself on your progress and perseverance.

During life's great challenges, an empowering intervention is to recall personal strengths. (Ivey & Ivey, 2007). Reflect on some strengths you've displayed during a challenging time in the past in which you've experienced loss. You can write about either an actual death or about a symbolic loss such as a job, a pet, a move, a friend, a promotion, a divorce, or any grievous experience in which you felt something was taken from you. As you spend time in thought, use the question set to focus on how you came through that life issue. Reflect on your gifts and assets. Recall what you're capable of accomplishing. This is a time to explore your positive personal resources as you formulate answers to the questions. Stay mindful of these resources, and draw from them as you continue to work through your grief.

■ Write about past experiences that come to mind. There may be more than one.

_____
_____
_____
_____
_____
_____
_____
_____
_____
_____
_____

Taking Steps in Loss and Life: Guided Reflections Journal

■ What personal strengths, assets, or gifts did you use during this time?

_____
_____
_____
_____
_____
_____

■ How did you come through this loss?

_____
_____
_____
_____
_____

■ What did you learn about yourself, about others, and about life?

_____
_____
_____
_____
_____

■ How have you grown through this experience?

_____
_____
_____
_____
_____
_____
_____
_____

■ How are you stronger because of the experience?

_____
_____
_____
_____
_____

■ What positive traits do you see in yourself that can be applied today to your grieving experience?

_____
_____
_____
_____
_____
_____
_____
_____
_____
_____
_____
_____
_____
_____

■ Write a kind note to yourself. Begin with this thought starter: *(Insert name), you are able to accomplish good things in life. You have some innate gifts and talents. Some of these are…* (Go on to write about these. No negativity allowed!)

_____
_____
_____
_____
_____

A Letter About Me

Interview someone you trust or someone who's close to you.
Ask them to write an encouraging letter about your strengths and character addressed to you.
Specifically, ask them to recall a time you worked through a difficulty, overcame an obstacle, or experienced a well-earned success in your life.
Attach the letter to the space below as a permanent part of your journal.
Read it whenever you need encouragement.

Danglers: Unfinished Business

The fifth task listed in *The Work of Renewal* is, "*Permit the death to redefine you in newness and growth, both inside and out*" (Hoy, 2007; Wolfelt, 2003; Worden, 2009). Danglers left unattended can be a major hindrance to accomplishing the tasks of grieving, especially this one. These types of thoughts can reside just below the level of conscious awareness and remain as an emotional stuck-place blocking the way of progress. Spend some time getting these to the surface where they can be managed. Address your writing to your loved one this week. This is a very intimate exercise that requires you to draw deeply from within yourself. The more you open your heart and pour it into your writings, the more effective the exercise (adapted from Grant, 1995; Neimeyer, 2012; Rich, 2001; Worden 2009).

In this reflection segment, you have the opportunity to address ideas, conversations, or situations you feel were left dangling between you and your loved one. What relationship or life areas remain unresolved that still need expressing? Write about things that needed understanding by either of you. Include experiences you wish your beloved could have had and experiences you wish you would not have encountered together. Additionally, think about addressing anything you wish your loved one knew about you or about your shared history. You can also add any new insights you've come upon since the death. You may want to tell your loved one about a ritual you're going to perform to honor his or her life.

Consider writing just a few sentences a day, as you feel comfortable. If you would like, when you're finished, read the letter aloud to your loved one or incorporate the letter into a ritual of memorializing. It's recommended you care for yourself with an emotion drawing afterwards.

Making Decisions

*T*his question set aids in continuing your work with the fifth task listed in *The Work of Renewal*: *Permit the death to re-define you in newness and growth, both inside and out* (Hoy, 2007; Wolfelt, 2003; Worden, 2009). While in *The Grief Realm*, decision making can be particularly difficult yet necessary. Transitioning through change requires some decisions be made. Change will involve moving away from certain elements while moving toward others.

This section is devoted to helping you clarify your thinking and helping you pinpoint priorities. Taking time to focus on decisions at hand and addressing at least some of these, restores a sense of order and self-confidence. Use the guiding questions below to sort your thoughts, make plans, and take action. Making decisions can involve a series of steps (collecting information, visiting with a trusted friend, making phone calls, looking at banking accounts, and so on). Breaking decisions down into smaller steps, writing them, and verbalizing them will help increase the likelihood that goals are accomplished. It's best to postpone making big decisions while you're still grieving. The drive to avoid pain and emptiness can impact sound judgment (Worden, 2009). Be sure to answer the questions and perform the activities only as you feel you're ready and able.

■ Begin by grouping decisions according to two criteria: what you'd like to move *away from* and what you'd like to *move toward*. First, spend time in thought considering what you may need to move *away from* and note your ideas in the space below. Stretch your thinking to include all five domains of your life: Spiritual, Physical, Emotional, Behavioral (Relational), and Mental (Thoughts).

_____
_____
_____
_____
_____
_____
_____

■ Now spend time giving attention to what you may need to *move toward* in the same five domains. Jot down everything that comes to mind.

_____
_____
_____
_____
_____
_____
_____
_____
_____
_____
_____

■ What are some of the most pressing choices/decisions you think you need to make right now? Put your thoughts in writing.

_____
_____
_____
_____
_____
_____
_____

■ Pick your top few (no more than three) most doable decisions, write them in the space below, and make them priorities.

_____
_____
_____
_____
_____
_____
_____
_____

■ Reframe your decisions into realistic, specific goals. Rewrite the sentence starter below, and personalize it with your thoughts. Do this for every decision you are facing right now in which you need some motivating and accountability. Written tasks are more likely to be completed! Writing gives power to thoughts by transforming them into something visual.

I will accomplish _____, by ____(when)_____ .

_____
_____
_____
_____
_____
_____
_____

■ Now write a series of action steps for each decision. What can you begin to do this week or even tomorrow toward setting these in motion? Make your action steps as small as you can to ensure you'll commit to doing them!

_____
_____
_____
_____
_____
_____
_____

■ Repeat this exercise for every future decision that arises. Post your goals in a place you can visit them regularly. Track your accomplishments in the space below. Think of some rewards you can give to yourself, and reward every success you encounter, no matter how small.

My Accomplishments and Rewards

_____
_____
_____
_____
_____
_____

My Accomplishments and Rewards

Write a Letter of Sympathy to Self
Write a Truce with Self

It's time to devote further effort toward engaging in holistic self-care with this reflection exercise. Surprisingly, one of the biggest obstacles to moving out of *The Grief Realm* can be found within ourselves. Emotions such as guilt and fear take hold and keep us in a grieving state. At times, our softer self and our demanding self are at odds. Have you found that you're capable of being your own worst judge, critic, or enemy? Consider this week, whether your demanding self is dominating or blocking your progress and oppressing you with strongholds of guilt, or some sort of self-condemnation.

■ Turn your compassion inward, and write a letter to the demanding self inside of you. Tell your demanding self you want to declare a truce! Let your heart guide you and speak out that you want to unite all energy toward self-kindness, as you move forward to face the future (Jackson, 1962). Expand on these thoughts and add observations of your self-talk and how you've been treating yourself. Recall instances in which you have been impatient or intolerant. Get yourself in full agreement with this truce and hold your demanding self accountable with gentle reminders. Vow things will be different as you progress.

_____
_____
_____
_____
_____
_____
_____
_____
_____
_____
_____
_____

■ What specific strongholds did you identify in confronting your demanding self? How effective was your confrontation? Use the truce to regulate these strongholds if they continue to arise as barriers to your healing. Read the truce aloud as much as is needed.

■ Now allow yourself to consider, what it will be like to live without the strongholds you confronted and described above. Describe your life and what you will feel like on the inside. What will be different? What will you leave behind? (Rich, 2001).

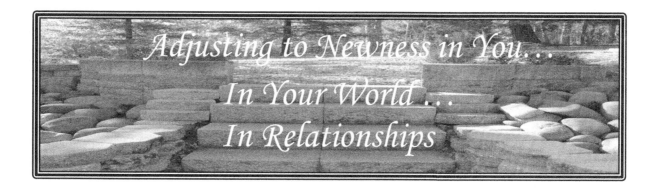

Once again you will revisit the fifth task here in this section of your journaling. Recall it is, *"Permit the death to re-define you in newness and growth, both inside and out"* (Hoy, 2007; Wolfelt, 2003; Worden, 2009).

Emotional healing after death has been likened to building a life around a hollow place in your heart (Worden, 2009). Might the notion be suggested that the hollow place does not have to remain empty? Might you consider it could be filled with the life energy or imprint of your loved one as you work to reshape and nurture the relationship in a new way? All the experiences, fond moments, passions, laughter, the challenges, the learning, the spiritual goodness, and all of the life shared are wrapped up in an everlasting, invisible force. It's part of you that resides in your special heart place. Part of the overall adjustment is found in adapting your self-concept to fit with your new place in life. Perhaps the greatest honor to your beloved is for you to blossom in your new life with the lasting effects of this beautiful energy. You're residing in the world with an enhanced presence for having experienced time with that person.

It has been said that love is the most powerful force in the universe. This goal of renewal is more than continuing to exist. It involves growth, refining, and ultimate re-defining from having shared life with someone you love and from having experienced loss. Take time to center on the questions below, and see if you can use your discoveries to polish perspectives.

■In what ways can you see yourself as a whole, autonomous individual again?

___
___
___
___
___
___
___
___

■ In what areas can you see new growth in your life, now and in your future?

_____
_____
_____
_____
_____
_____
_____

■ To which areas of life can you redirect the love energy you continue to feel for your beloved?

_____
_____
_____
_____
_____
_____
_____

■ Into what can you pour this love energy?

_____
_____
_____
_____
_____
_____
_____
_____
_____
_____

Moving Ahead

The *Moving Ahead* question set is designed to propel your thinking beyond the grieving process (Rich, 2001; Worden 2009). Nurturing thoughts that move you mentally beyond where you're thinking and feeling right now, create momentum in a future direction (Worden, 2009). Some of you may not be ready to move past grieving while some of you are closer to completing this task. Regardless of where you are in your grieving process, be encouraged that moving past pain does not mean you'll be forgetting your loved one (Wolfelt, 2003; Worden, 2009). Truly, it's quite the opposite. In using this guide and in doing the work these past weeks, you've been honoring and memorializing your beloved with a good deal of energy. You're working toward keeping "the door to their life open" (as cited in Hickman, 1994). Understanding is not a necessary prerequisite for acknowledging the mysteries of life. Instead, we learn to live with them and around them. Allowing ourselves to continue to experience lasting joy and memories affirms the life even after death. See what positive ideas you might come away with as you give thoughtful consideration to the questions.

■ What do the words *moving ahead* mean to you? Be as detailed as possible in your answer as you think on moving ahead in the five domains of humanness:

Spiritual, Physical, Emotional, Behavioral (Relational), and Mental (Thinking)

_____
_____
_____
_____
_____
_____
_____
_____
_____

■ Does moving ahead involve making changes? If so, what are the changes you are facing? If you need to make decisions to implement positive change, use the *Making Decisions* section to guide you in working through these.

■ Write down ideas of how you might introduce newness into your life. Think of activities, people, education, skills, hobbies, pets, and creativity. Is there even something very small that would enhance your life? Decide which of the ideas would be the easiest to begin.

■ Extend your possibilities and think of desires that have always been with you. Reach far back to early in your life; maybe even to when you were a child. Is there a dream that went unanswered, an event that was never attended, a skill that was never developed, or a desire that was never explored? What thoughts do you sense trickling?

_____
_____
_____
_____
_____
_____
_____

■ Choose one or two of your ideas that seem the most doable right now and tuck the rest away for a little while. What kind of help might you need to get started? What steps do you need to take to make your ideas a reality?

_____
_____
_____
_____
_____
_____

■ Let yourself consider, even for a little while, what it would be like to move past your grieving and exit *The Grief Realm*. What awaits you on the other side?

_____
_____
_____
_____
_____
_____
_____
_____
_____

My Future Life

Create a miniature collage. Find some small pictures or clip art that best represent a few things you would like to see in your future. Paste these in the space below.
Creating a visual depiction of your hopes adds strength to your ideas.
You may want to begin with just a few, and add to these in the days ahead.

Reflections Revisited

*T*he effort you're putting into your self-reflection is commendable! It's often beneficial to re-visit some of the questions in the sets. As you progress through *The Grief Realm* with increased awareness, new memories and thoughts will surface. Take a moment to review your work thus far. Note any additional reflections in the space provided. It might be helpful to reference the page number of the questions energizing your writings.

_____
_____
_____
_____
_____
_____
_____
_____
_____
_____
_____
_____
_____
_____
_____
_____
_____
_____
_____

Emotion Drawing Section

The pages in this section have been provided for your drawings. Be sure to refer to the instructions at the beginning of the journal before you begin.

APPENDICES

The appendices which follow have been created by the authors. They are a small part of a collection of tools created for use in the Taking Steps in Loss and Life Grief Support Group. The entire tool set can be found in the grief support group facilitator's manual.

Taking Steps in Loss and Life: Guided Reflections Journal

Appendix A
The Grief Realm
(Things that hurt, Things to restore, Things to discover, Things to accomplish)

EXIT PORTAL

Restoration   Renewal   Peacefulness

Permit the death to redefine you   Adjust to newness

Balance   Laughter   Love   Relationships   Courage   Moving beyond

Examining self   Self-expression   Choices

Relief   Decision   Finding meaning

Self-reflection   Nurturing   Perspective shaping   Self-Care

Self-devaluing   Frustration   Irritable   Stomach Pain   Challenged Beliefs

Fear   Distrust   Anxiety   Regrets   Unfinished Business

Reshape and nurture the bond in your heart and memories

Headaches   Guilt   Fatigue   Resentment   Victimized   Loneliness

Examine the grief wound   Process the pain

Pain   Withdrawal   Forgetfulness   Short-tempered   Disinterest   Hallucinations
Apathy

Coping skills   Hope   Support   Memorializing

Preoccupation   Fear   Heart palpitations   Depression   Substance use   Self-neglect

Allow the certainty of the death

Aimlessness   Restlessness   Disorganization   Dreams   Searching and not finding

Anguish   Depersonalization   Meaninglessness   Dread   Clinging

Shock   Disorientation   Disbelief   Confusion   Anger   Detached   Shut down

Yearning   Crying   Exhaustion   Appetite loss

ENTRANCE PORTAL

© 2013 Barbette Shepherd

Appendix B

Comforting Scriptures

Deuteronomy 31:8

Jeremiah 1:8

Lamentations 3:25

Micah 7:7

Psalm 27:1

Psalm 23:4

Psalm 119:76

Proverbs 3:24

Isaiah 49:13

Isaiah 12:2

Isaiah 57:1-2

Matthew 5:4

Mark 5:36

Luke 12:7

John 14:27

Romans 15:13

Appendix C

Be Quiet Death!!

You have taken a body, Death, but you cannot take the life lived!

It was left behind imprinted on time, and on minds,

The value of every life, no matter how long, outweighs your strike, Death

It is life that will be remembered

The music

The tears

The writings

The expressions

The patter of feet

The experiences

The shouts

The laughter

The kindness

The kisses

The accomplishments

The energy

The hiccups

The angry protests

The hugs

The songs

The words

The love

The eternal essence

This life is now joined to other lives and joined to time

Death I defy you! You will take no more!

You are but a tool to open the door

To a new beginning

© 2013 Barbette Shepherd

About the Authors

Barbette and Randy both have long histories of investing in the lives of others. Their faith is pivotal to all they endeavor. The caring, positive natures they possess blend effectively into their personal and professional relationships. As a team, they dedicate a portion of their lives to ministry and to coaching their clients toward a renewed existence as they transition through change in life. Their credentials are evidence of specialty training that equips them with unique skills and insights characteristic of their services. Barbette holds a bachelor's and master's degree in psychology and has attained certification as a grief counselor. Randy holds a master's degree in nursing education with emphasis on holistic wellness and grief. Each author has been certified as a professional life coach.

Their home is tucked away in the mountains where they're fortunate to spend time in sanctuary. Careers, work, and recreation fill their time with daily challenges and rewards. In the rough patches of life, they turn to God and to each other for guidance and support. Family, friends, and pets are prevailing sources of love and goodness.

The collective writings by Barbette and Randy, both published and unpublished, are primarily aimed at personal reflection and inspiring others on their own journey of self-discovery, spirituality, and growth. Much of Barbette's work has been used in the school system and in colleges, for which she has written and adapted active learning curricula. The authors invite you to visit their website, LifeSteps: Shepherds' Integrative Services: www.lifesteps.us.

"He that conceals his grief finds no remedy for it"
(Anonymous, 2011).

References

Anonymous (2011). *He that conceals his grief.* Retrieved from www.grievingdads.wordpress.com

Genn, R. (2013). *Art quotes: The painter's keys resource of art quotations.* Retrieved from http://clicks.robertgenn.com

Grant, A.C.(1995). *The healing journey: Manual for a grief support group.* New Jersey: Vista Publishing.

Hickman, M.W. (1994). *Healing after loss: Daily meditations for working through grief.* New York: Harper Collins Publishers.

Hoy, W.G. (2007). *Guiding people through grief: How to start and lead bereavement support groups.* Dallas: Compass Press.

Ivey, A.E. & Ivey, M.B. (2007). *Intentional interviewing and counseling* (6th ed.). Belmont, CA: Thomson Brooks/Cole.

Jackson, E.N. (1962). *You and your grief.* New York: Hawthorn books, Inc.

Kubler-Ross, E. (1969). *On death and dying.* New York: Macmillan.

Neimeyer, R.A. (2012). *Techniques of grief therapy.* New York. Routledge.

Rich, P. (2001). *Grief counseling homework planner.* New York: John Wiley and Sons, Inc.

Shepherd, B. (2013). *The parable of the gardener: For those who grieve.* Publisher: Author.

Shepherd, B. & Shepherd, R. (2013). *Taking steps in loss and life: A grief support group manual.* Publisher: Authors.

Wolfelt, A. (2003). *Understanding your grief.* Colorado: Companion Press.

Worden, J. W. (2009). *Grief counseling and grief therapy: A handbook for the mental health practitioner.* New York: Springer Publishing Co.

Made in the USA
Coppell, TX
18 March 2023

14258576R00044